discovermore

Exploring Primary Sources

Exploring the Magna Carta

Sarah Schmidtt

Britannica Educational Publishing

IN ASSOCIATION WITH

THE ROSEN PUBLISHING GROUP

Published in 2025 by Britannica Educational Publishing (a trademark of Encyclopædia Britannica, Inc.)
in association with The Rosen Publishing Group, Inc.
2544 Clinton Street, Buffalo, NY 14224

Distributed exclusively by Rosen Publishing.
To see additional Britannica Educational Publishing titles, go to rosenpublishing.com.

Editor: Brianna Propis
Cover Design: Michael Flynn
Interior Design: Rachel Rising

Photo Credits: Cover Jimlop collection / Alamy Stock Photo; Cover (series background) Dai Yim/Shutterstock.com; p. 4 https://commons.wikimedia.org/wiki/File:Magna_Carta_(1297_version,_Parliament_House,_Canberra,_Australia)_-_20080416.jpg; p. 5 https://en.m.wikipedia.org/wiki/File:Surrender_of_Lord_Cornwallis.jpg; p. 7 https://en.m.wikipedia.org/wiki/File:Magna_Carta_King_John_signing_the_Magna_Carta_reluctantly_by_Michael,_Arthur_C_(d_1945).jpg; p. 8 https://en.wikipedia.org/wiki/File:William_Shakespeare_by_John_Taylor,_edited.jpg; p. 9 Traceyaphotos2/Shutterstock.com; p. 10 https://commons.wikimedia.org/wiki/File:British_School_-_King_John_-_Google_Art_Project.jpg; p. 11 https://en.m.wikipedia.org/wiki/File:Reeve_and_Serfs.jpg; p. 13 https://commons.wikimedia.org/wiki/File:A_Chronicle_of_England_-_Page_222_-_The_Barons_Swear_to_Achieve_Their_Liberties.jpg; p. 15 https://en.wikipedia.org/wiki/File:Flag_of_medieval_France.png; p. 15 Buncha Lim/Shutterstock.com; p. 17 Everett Collection/Shutterstock.com; p. 18 Dave Carroll/Shutterstock.com; p. 19 https://en.m.wikipedia.org/wiki/File:John_of_England_vs_Louis_VIII_of_France.jpg; p. 20 https://en.m.wikipedia.org/wiki/File:Stephenlangtonstatuecanterburycathedraloutside.jpg; p. 21 Alexey Fedorenko/Shutterstock.com; p. 23 Hesketh Road Photography/Shutterstock.com; p. 23 https://commons.wikimedia.org/wiki/File:Elizabeth_I_in_Parliament.jpg; p. 24 Viorel Sima/Shutterstock.com; p. 25 ungvar/Shutterstock.com; p. 26 Michael Tubi/Shutterstock.com; p. 27 Mistervlad/Shutterstock.com; p. 28 dpa picture alliance / Alamy Stock Photo; p. 29 Kauka Jarvi/Shutterstock.com.

Library of Congress Cataloging-in-Publication Data
Names: Schmidtt, Sarah, author.
Title: Exploring the Magna Carta / Sarah Schmidtt.
Description: Buffalo : Britannica Educational Publishing, an imprint of Rosen Publishing, [2025] | Series: Discover more: exploring primary sources | Includes index.
Identifiers: LCCN 2024038021 | ISBN 9781641903813 (library binding) | ISBN 9781641903806 (paperback) | ISBN 9781641903820 (ebook)
Subjects: LCSH: Magna Carta--Juvenile literature.
Classification: LCC JN147 .S36 2025 | DDC 942.03/3--dc23/eng/20240823
LC record available at https://lccn.loc.gov/2024038021

Manufactured in the United States of America

CPSIA Compliance Information: Batch #CWBRIT25. For further information contact Rosen Publishing at 1-800-237-9932.

Contents

Rules and Laws

What would you do if there were no rules? It may sound like fun because having no rules means you can do whatever you want. But without rules, people can also steal or hurt one another without consequences. Society could become unsafe and unfair. Rules exist to protect people.

All modern governments have sets of rules known as laws. These laws are usually written down as documents, so people know what they are. Governments did not always have written laws. One of the earliest examples in history of a government's written laws is the Magna Carta, which is Latin for Great **Charter**. This document was signed over 800 years ago in England.

Only four copies of the original Magna Carta documents exist today.

The Magna Carta inspired Americans during the American Revolution.

The story of the Magna Carta begins with a disliked king and headstrong nobles. In spite of its age, the Magna Carta remains an influential document in history and was even studied by countries such as the United States to make their own laws.

WORD WISE

A CHARTER IS A DOCUMENT ISSUED BY THE GOVERNMENT THAT GIVES OR LIMITS RIGHTS TO A GROUP.

Put It in Writing

The Magna Carta was a charter that granted certain rights to the people of England. Putting those rights down in writing was important for two reasons. First, the Magna Carta created an agreement between the king of England and his people. By writing down the laws, everyone knew what the laws were. People could point to the written laws if a disagreement came up. The Magna Carta meant that the king could no longer make up new laws whenever he wanted. Instead, even the king had to follow the rules written in the Magna Carta. It was the first official document stating that citizens had rights—not just the king.

Consider This

Why is it important that the king couldn't make up new laws whenever he wanted? Why would a ruler having unlimited power be dangerous for citizens?

On June 12, 1215, King John signed the Magna Carta.

Another reason it's so important that the Magna Carta was written down is because historians are now able to study it as a **primary source**. How else would historians today know how England's government worked back in 1215? We would only know about England's early laws and history from stories that were retold over time. When people tell stories instead of writing things down, there can be several versions of what really happened. Sadly, many things would be forgotten. But documents such as the Magna Carta and other primary sources help us to have a more objective, exact idea of what happened.

William Shakespeare's play, *King John*, is a secondary source about King John of England.

William Shakespeare

The Magna Carta was unusual because it was not offered by the king to his nobles, but rather demanded by the nobles from the king.

WORD WISE

A PRIMARY SOURCE IS A WRITTEN DOCUMENT OR OTHER SOURCE OF FIRSTHAND INFORMATION (SUCH AS A PHOTOGRAPH) DATING BACK TO THE TIME OR EVENT BEING STUDIED. THE MAGNA CARTA IS A PRIMARY SOURCE, WHILE A BOOK ABOUT THE MAGNA CARTA WOULD BE CONSIDERED A SECONDARY SOURCE.

Unlimited Power

England was an **absolute monarchy** from its founding in 886 until the early 1200s. From 1199 until 1216, it was ruled by King John. As king, John could declare whatever laws he wanted. He made English people fight in many wars and collected taxes from the people to pay for them.

At that time, England also had a social system called feudalism. Under feudalism, powerful people called nobles or lords built large estates and protected people who lived on their land. In return, the people the nobles protected, called serfs, farmed the nobles' land. The king of a country protected all the nobles. The nobles provided money and services to the king to pay him for protection.

King John

In an absolute monarchy, King John held unlimited power over the people of England.

In feudalism, serfs became property of their lord and were heavily controlled by them.

Without written laws or rights for the people living in England, King John could treat the English nobles (called barons) badly. The barons then treated the people who worked for them badly.

WORD WISE

AN ABSOLUTE MONARCHY IS A TYPE OF GOVERNMENT THAT GIVES ITS RULER—A KING OR A QUEEN—UNLIMITED POWER.

The King of England

King John was born in England in 1166. When his brother, King Richard I, died in 1199, John became king of England. England's barons, church leaders, and the common people disliked John. He demanded a lot of money from them in the form of taxes. He also argued with the leaders of the Roman Catholic Church, which was very powerful in England at the time.

One reason John demanded high taxes from his people was for a series of wars he fought with France. In 1200, John married a French woman named Isabella. However, Isabella was supposed to marry a French noble named Hugh IX of Lusignan. (The Lusignans were a French noble family.) This made the Lusignans angry. To settle the matter, John was ordered to appear before King Philip II of France. Philip II declared a war to take John's land in France after John failed to appear before him.

Many of England's barons and the Catholic Church thought King John was cruel and selfish.

Consider This

Sometimes serfs had to be soldiers during war. During an age of feudalism, how do you think nobles felt about a king who declared war?

Under the feudal system, the English barons had to provide money and troops to John in times of war. War is very expensive. However, John kept demanding more money and troops from the barons. By 1206, John had lost several territories that he had held in France. The barons became angry that they were losing money and troops.

In a monarchy, the people do not vote for their rulers. Kings and queens inherit their power. The people support them because they are strong, powerful leaders. However, after France defeated England, John looked weak. Several years into John's reign, the barons lost their patience with the king. They felt it was time for a change, and they were ready to demand it.

compare and contrast

The United States is a democracy. In a democracy, people vote for who they want to lead the government. How is a democracy different from a monarchy? Are they similar in any ways?

During King John's reign, England fought expensive wars in France—and lost.

Some barons who refused to pay King John's taxes were imprisoned, along with members of their families.

The barons had to figure out how to limit John's power. They were tired of paying such high taxes. They could have fought a war against John to take away his power. However, these nobles were already tired of spending money and sending troops to fight wars. Waging war against the king would cost them even more money. They did not want to fight unless they had to.

Instead of trying to remove John from power, the barons wrote a list of rules and rights. They wanted John to follow the rules, which would limit his power. They also wanted him to respect their rights. This written list of laws and rights became the Magna Carta.

Consider This

The barons decided to make King John sign a list of rules rather than find a new king altogether. Why do you think they did this? Do you think finding a new king would have solved their problems in the same way?

The Articles of the Barons was a list of demands and reformations that formed the basis of the Magna Carta.

The barons knew they had to force John to sign the Magna Carta, so a group of the nobles began a **rebellion** against him. John did not like what the Magna Carta said, but he was too weak to resist the barons. If John did not sign the Magna Carta, the barons would overthrow him. So, John agreed to sign the charter. He signed the document at Runnymede on the River Thames in June 1215. However, John continued to fight the barons, and the argument led to a civil war. John died in October 1216 during the civil war.

The Magna Carta guaranteed that the king would respect feudal rights and privileges, maintaining the freedom of the church, and honor the nation's laws.

The First Barons' War was a civil war in England between King John and a group of rebellious barons. The war broke out in 1215.

The Magna Carta became the basis for English law. It had sixty-three sections called clauses. These clauses were meant to protect the rights of the church and the English barons. However, the ideas in the Magna Carta reached beyond England. The leaders of many other countries used the charter to help them form their own laws.

WORD WISE

A REBELLION IS AN ORGANIZED EFFORT BY A GROUP OF PEOPLE TO CHANGE OR OVERTHROW THE LEADER OR GOVERNMENT OF A COUNTRY.

A Free Church

The Magna Carta's first clause dealt with freedom of the church. During his reign, John tried to tell the leaders of the Roman Catholic Church in England how the church should be run. Often, the church leaders disagreed with John. John punished them by taking their property and money.

Stephen Langston

Archbishop Stephen Langston played an important role in securing the freedom of the church. He advised and supported the barons' opposition to King John.

The freedom of the church in England continues today.

In Clause One, the Magna Carta says, "The English church shall be free, and shall have its rights undiminished and its liberties unimpaired." This means the government could not take away any of the church's rights or its freedoms. The king could no longer take the church's money for his own uses.

This clause did not apply to King John only. The clause says that the church's freedom will exist "for us and our heirs for ever." This means that the rights listed in the Magna Carta were intended to exist forever.

Consider This

Should the government be allowed to take money from the church? Why or why not?

Fair Taxation

Before the Magna Carta, the king was able to demand any taxes he wanted from his people. However, Clause Twelve of the Magna Carta says, "No scutage or aid shall be imposed in our kingdom unless by common counsel of our kingdom." ("Scutage" and "aid" refer to taxes.) This means the barons had to agree that taxes were fair. If they didn't, the king could not collect the money.

Clause Fourteen explains how the barons and church leaders would decide if taxes are fair or not. These two clauses became the basis for the idea of the Parliament, which is the law-making group in England's government.

The Magna Carta ensured the king could not collect taxes without the barons's approval.

compareandcontrast

Why was it important that the barons had to agree if taxes were fair? Why is it helpful to have a group of people make a decision rather than one person?

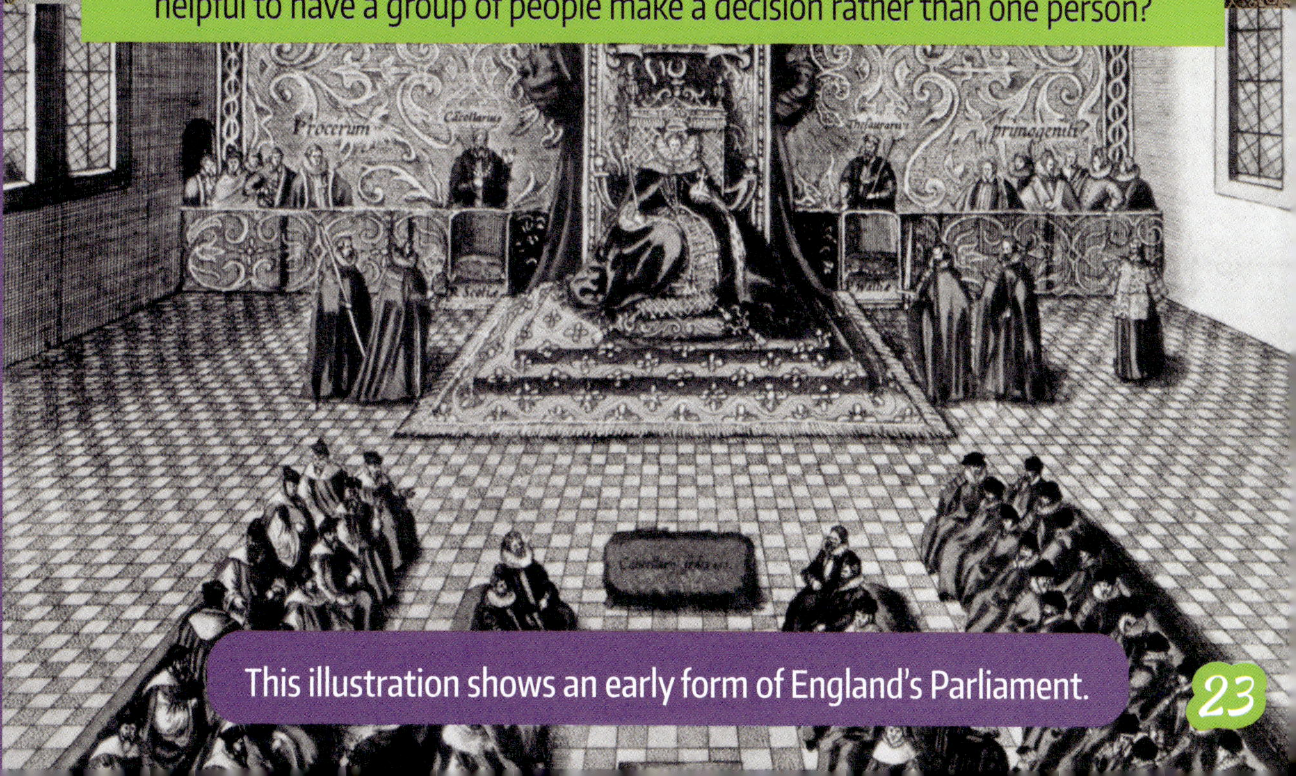

This illustration shows an early form of England's Parliament.

Improving the Justice System

Another power the king held before the Magna Carta was his ability to arrest and punish anybody he wanted. Several clauses of the Magna Carta protect people from being arrested or punished for no reason.

Clause Twenty says that a person can only be punished "in accordance with the degree of the offence." This means a person could not be sent to jail for a long time or put to death for a small crime. Furthermore, Clause Thirty-Eight says that a person can't be put on trial without "reliable witnesses" who can give evidence.

Punishments for crimes were often cruel and unfair before the Magna Carta.

The writers of the U.S. Bill of Rights were inspired by the Magna Carta when forming rules for the U.S. justice system. They wrote, "No person shall be held to answer for a . . . crime, unless on a presentment or indictment of a grand jury."

Clause Thirty-Nine is one of the most important clauses in the charter. It says, "No free man shall be arrested or imprisoned . . . except by the lawful judgment of his peers." This means that a group of people—similar in status to the person convicted—must agree the person actually committed a crime before sending them to prison.

Consider This

Nowadays, it is standard in many countries to have witnesses of a crime testify, or explain what they saw, before someone is convicted. Why is it important for witnesses to testify before someone is convicted of a crime?

An Influential Document

The Magna Carta is more than an eight-hundred-year-old set of rules and laws—it is a piece of living history. Many of the clauses of the Magna Carta influenced laws that still exist today. The **American Founding Fathers** were inspired by it as they made documents that laid the foundation for the United States.

Today, England is a part of the United Kingdom. England is still a monarchy, but the powers of the king and queen remain limited thanks to the Magna Carta. Some members of the country's Parliament are voted for by the people of England, while others are nobles and church leaders.

The current monarch of England is King Charles III.

Today, the people of England elect six hundred and fifty members of Parliament to represent their interests.

WORD WISE

AMERICA'S FOUNDING FATHERS WERE INFLUENTIAL POLITICAL LEADERS DURING THE AMERICAN REVOLUTION AND THE FORMATION OF THE UNITED STATES. THEY INCLUDED GEORGE WASHINGTON, THOMAS JEFFERSON, JOHN ADAMS, BENJAMIN FRANKLIN, ALEXANDER HAMILTON, JOHN JAY, AND JAMES MADISON.

During the 1700s, the Founding Fathers borrowed many of the Magna Carta's ideas for the U.S. Constitution. The basic freedoms and rights of individual citizens, including the right to a fair trial, were borrowed directly from the Magna Carta.

Given the Magna Carta is over eight hundred years old, it's hard to imagine original copies still exist. Four of them remain today, and they are carefully protected so that they can continue to survive.

The surviving copies are on display in museums for people to visit.

There is a monument at the location of the Magna Carta's signing in England today.

In 2015, the four surviving documents were brought together for the eight hundredth anniversary of the Magna Carta's signing. They were displayed in the British Parliament building for the public. The legacy of the document and the inspiration it gave to the foundation of many nations has resulted in historians studying it for many centuries and more to come.

Consider This

How might the U.S. and English governments be different today if the Magna Carta never existed?

Glossary

archbishop A senior bishop, or high-ranking member of the Christian clergy, who oversees all bishops and priests in a particular area.

constitution A document listing the main laws of a country or group, including the powers of the government and the rights of the people.

counsel Advice given to someone.

document A written or printed paper giving information about or proof of something.

evidence Material presented to a court to help find the truth in a matter.

firsthand Coming directly from the original source.

indictment A formal charge or accusation of a serious crime.

inherit To receive something (for example, money, property, or a title) from someone when that person dies.

overthrow To remove someone or something from power, especially by force.

presentment A formal presentation of information in court.

reign The authority or rule of a monarch.

For More Information

Books

Brown, Don. *We the People!* New York, NY: Amulet Books, 2022.

Lüsted, Marcia Amidon. *The Magna Carta.* North Mankato, MN: Capstone, 2020.

Trusiani, Lisa. *The History of the Constitution.* Emeryville, CA: Rockridge Press, 2021.

Websites

Britannica Kids: Magna Carta
kids.britannica.com/students/article/Magna-Carta/275610
Read more about the charter that changed world governments forever.

Britannica Kids: Parliament
kids.britannica.com/kids/article/parliament/353600#:~:text=Parliament%20is%20the%20legislature%2C%20or,in%20separate%20branches%20of%20government.
Learn more about the English law-making body, Parliament.

British Library: What Is Magna Carta?
www.youtube.com/watch?v=7xo4tUMdAMw
Review the importance and development of the Magna Carta with this video.

Publisher's note to educators and parents: Our editors have carefully reviewed these websites to ensure that they are suitable for students. Many websites change frequently, however, and we cannot guarantee that a site's future contents will continue to meet our high standards of quality and educational value. Be advised that students should be closely supervised whenever they access the internet.

Index